W9-ASU-253

Say It Again!
501 Wacky Word Puzzles from Highlights

Illustrated by Mike Dammer

Highlights Press
Honesdale, Pennsylvania

Copyright © 2013 by Highlights for Children, Inc.

All rights reserved.

For information about permission to reproduce selections from this book, please contact permissions@highlights.com.

Highlights for Children, Inc.

P.O. Box 18201

Columbus, Ohio 43218-0201

highlightspress.com

Printed in the United States of America

ISBN: 978-1-62091-072-6

Library of Congress Control Number: 2013933040

First edition

Visit our website at highlights.com.

10 9 8 7 6 5 4

Design by Cynthia Faber Smith

Production by Margaret Mosomillo

The titles are set in Aachen.

The text is set in Bones.

Additional Art

David Helton: pages 2, 16, 20, 37, 51, 53, 55, 57, 61, 64, 84, 128, 137, 151, 156, 157, 163, 177, 180, 189, 193, 203, 208, 214, 217

Andi Butler: pages 6, 42, 114, 116, 226, 229

Pete Whitehead: pages 23, 67, 123

David Coulson: pages 47, 74, 171

Jim Steck: pages 69, 107, 231

Hey Kids!: pages 95, 140, 147, 174, 210, 219, 225

Puzzling Words You'll Find Inside

Anagram
A word or phrase made by mixing up the letters of another word or phrase
Example: a gentleman / elegant man

Homonym
Two words that sound the same but have different meanings
Example: ate / eight

Onomatopoeia
A word that sounds like what it means
Example: buzz

Oxymoron
A combination of words with opposite meanings
Example: jumbo shrimp

Palindrome
A word or phrase that reads the same backward or forward
Example: go dog

Spoonerism
A mix-up of the first sounds or letters of two or more words
Example: tip of the slung / slip of the tongue

Oh, Onomatopoeias

murmur

eek

achoo

boom

plop

squeak

hiccup

What's the Word?

Flip every other letter to read a message.

L E T T E R S C A N B E S T R A N G E

Picture Puzzler

What tasty snack does this picture represent?

Tongue Twisters

Betty and Bob brought back blue balloons from the big bazaar.

Will walks on the red rock wall.

Peter Piper picked a peck of pickled peppers.

Answers on page 235

3

Palindromes, Please

In words, alas,
drown I.

Madam, I'm Adam.

Evil Olive

Never odd or even

Ma has a ham.

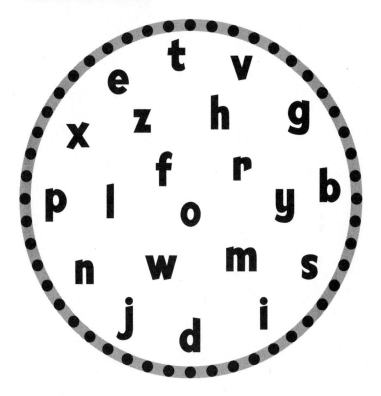

Use the letters of the alphabet that are missing from the circle to find a barnyard sound.

Answers on page 235

Can you name these
sports terms?

Unscramble the letters to find out what's for dinner.

opus

coat

west

takes

hilic

ladsa

regrub

rist-yfr

Answers on page 235

freer dends

My zips are lipped.

fighting a liar

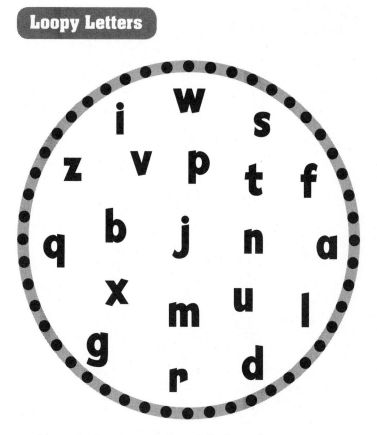

Use the letters of the alphabet that are missing from the circle to find a team sport.

Answers on page 235

We started with *snake* and changed one letter at a time, each time creating a new word, to turn it into a *shark*:

SNAKE

SHAKE

SHARE

SHARK

Now, can you change DOGS into CATS?

DOGS

_ _ _ _

_ _ _ _

CATS

Answers on page 235

Pen Pals by Anita Letterback

Don't Jump to Conclusions
by Megan Assumption

How to Pet an Alligator by B. Careful

The Water's Surface by Al G.

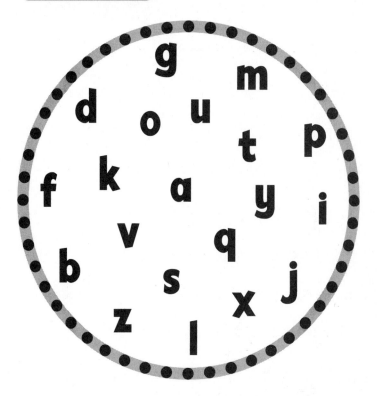

Use the letters of the alphabet that are missing from the circle to find a tool.

Answers on page 235

Read this aloud as fast as you can.

Betty Botter had some butter,

"But," she said, "this butter's bitter.

If I bake this bitter butter,

It would make my batter bitter.

But a bit of better butter,

That would make my batter better."

So she bought a bit of butter—

Better than her bitter butter—

And she baked it in her batter;

And the batter was not bitter.

So 'twas better Betty Botter

Bought a bit of better butter.

What is stranger than seeing a catfish?

What's the difference between here and there?

What word has the most letters in it?

Answers on page 235

runny babbit

wave the sails

had as a matter

shoving leopard

Answers on page 235

Ew, eat a ewe?

a nut for a jar of tuna

Is it I? It is I!

to idiot

Todd erases a red dot.

llama mall

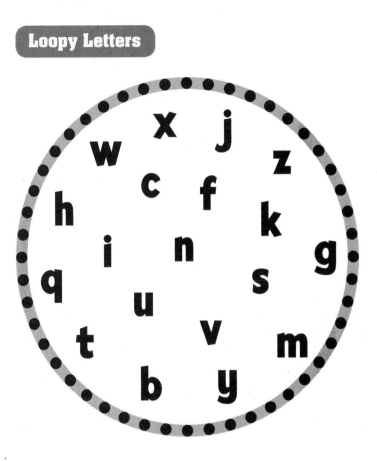

Use the letters of the alphabet that are missing from the circle to find a big cat.

Answers on page 235

Can you name these capital cities—and their countries?

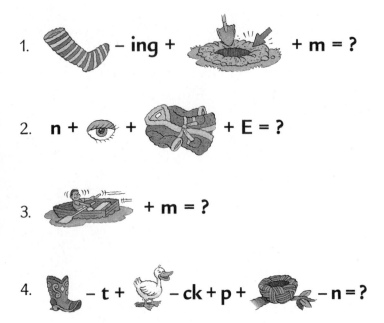

1. [worm] – ing + [hole] + m = ?

2. n + [eye] + [robe] + E = ?

3. [rowboat] + m = ?

4. [boot] – t + [goose] – ck + p + [nest] – n = ?

What do H, I, and M have in common that they don't share with S, B, or O?

What do H, I, S, and O have in common that they don't share with M, A, or T?

Answers on page 236

Not in a house, a school, a factory, or a person,

Nor in the outdoors or anywhere in nature,

I can be found in every building, in any city, and just once in your nation.

Read that third line again. I just told you the answer. What am I?

iT'S Me!

Picture Puzzler

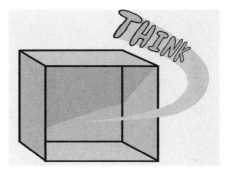

Laugh Library

Increase Your Luck! by Flora Leif-Clover

Never Too Late by Ida Star, Ted Sooner

Gardening for Beginners by Uneeda Seed

Time to Harvest by Tom Ayto and Brock Ali

Answers on page 236

Can you match the animals to their correct group names?

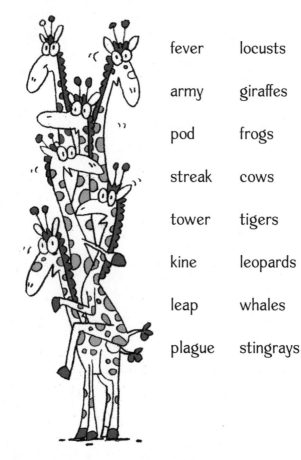

fever	locusts
army	giraffes
pod	frogs
streak	cows
tower	tigers
kine	leopards
leap	whales
plague	stingrays

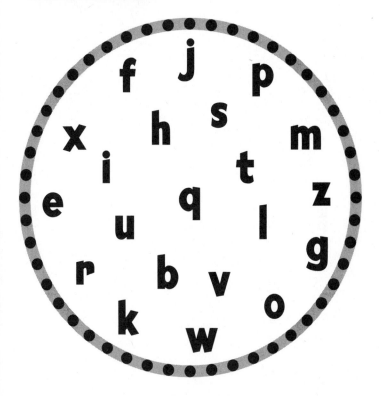

Use the letters of the alphabet that are
missing from the circle to find a sweet treat.

Answers on page 236

What letter makes each design?

1.

2.

3.

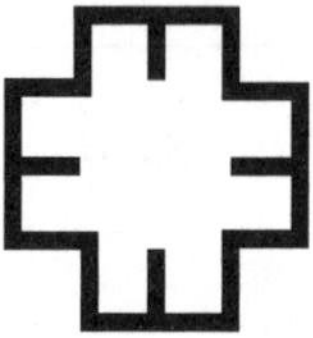

4.

Be Prepared by Justin Case

Getting Out of Debt by I. O. Millions

Pirate Secrets by Barry D. Treasure

Famous Nursery Rhymes by Pat E. Cake

Answers on page 236

What's the Word?

*Can you spot
the state name
in each sentence?*

Our newsletter
always comes
out weekly,
never monthly.

Is your cousin
Al a skater
or a surfer?

While trying to get the ends to
connect, I cut my finger.

Tony owns a beagle, a lab, a malamute, and a poodle.

You said to go north, Carol. I navigated correctly.

Uh-oh. I opened Mary's letter by mistake.

Answers on page 236

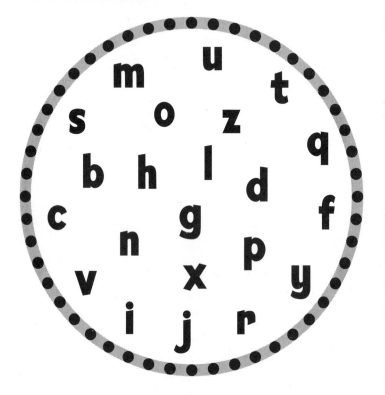

Use the letters of the alphabet that are missing from the circle to find a word that rhymes with beak.

Laugh Library

Check Your Homework by R. U. Wright

Old-Time Travel by Orson Cart

Uninteresting Tales by I. M. Yawning

Breakfast Favorites by Chris P. Bacon

How to Cut Down Trees by Tim Ber

Answers on page 236

jumbo shrimp

pretty ugly

deafening silence

clearly confused

Scrambled Words

Unscramble the letters to find the sports.

netins

fatlobol

ceraosls

aleblbas

eohykc

crocse

matssygnic

yllvoellab

nwmmisgi

akbslltaeb

akrtae

Answers on page 236

Can you think of any words that rhyme with the words below?

Month

Orange

Silver

Purple

I have five letters.
If you take away the first, middle, and last,
I will sound the same as before.
What am I?

eleven plus two = twelve plus one

the Morse code = here come dots

a gentleman = elegant man

Answers on page 237

schoolmaster = the classroom

dormitory = dirty room

the eyes = they see

Happy Homonyms

aisle	I'll	isle
buy	by	bye
way	weigh	whey
oar	or	ore
their	there	they're
chilly	Chile	chili

Picture Puzzler

Answers on page 237

How to Draw by Mark Er

Math by Adam Up

How to Brush Your Teeth by Dee Cay

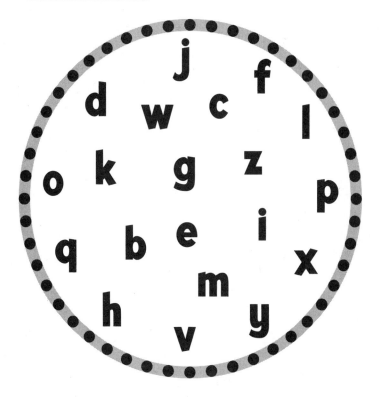

Use the letters of the alphabet that are
missing from the circle to find a planet
with rings.

Answers on page 237

Oops, Oxymorons

mild hot sauce

peace force

rolling stop

same difference

only choice

boneless ribs

good grief

definite maybe

Sleep

Can you name . . .

Something that comes in the mail and is also a boy's name?

A color that is also a fruit?

A part of your finger that is also used by a carpenter?

Something found on a shoe that may also be used to decorate a dress?

Something you wear that also refers to paint?

Answers on page 237

Six silky swans swam in the sticky swamp.

Breaking black bricks

Bold bald Bill builds big blue buildings.

Use the letters of the alphabet that are missing from the circle to find a vacation spot.

Answers on page 237

Can you find a sound-alike for each word?

peak

aloud

poor

bite

flu

close

one

horse

some

plain

Answers on page 237

What is the only English word for a number
that when spelled, its letters are in
alphabetical order?

What letter is nine inches long?

I start with the letter e,
I end with the letter e.
I contain only one letter,
Yet I am not the letter e!
What am I?

I know a word of letters three. Add two,
and fewer there will be.

How can you spell candy with two letters?

Oops, Oxymorons

awfully nice

almost exactly

even odds

silent scream

grow smaller

clever fool

Answers on page 237

49

roaring pain

candle with hair

eye ball

lead of spite

Answers on pages 237–238

Wacky Words

Have you ever had any of these
silly-sounding foods?

horned melon

popcorn shrimp

white chocolate

baked Alaska

hush puppies

buffalo wings

sour candy

chili spaghetti

All these words have the letters CAN in them. Use the clues to figure them out.

A yellow pet bird   CAN _ _ _

Lava pours out of this.   _ _ _ CAN _

It lights up a birthday cake.   CAN _ _ _

A type of nut   _ _ CAN

A narrow boat   CAN _ _

Picture Puzzler

Answers on page 238

four-legged tripod

long summary

gourmet cat food

constant change

instant classic

Answers on page 238

55

Palindromes, Please

Each sentence contains a palindrome. Can you spot them?

The pan turned redder the hotter it got.

Yesterday we took the kayak onto the lake and it sank.

"There is a problem with the rotator," the pilot said. "The flight will be delayed."

Picture Puzzlers

Answers on page 238

A reasonable fee to charge a bus passenger would be fair fare. Can you name a pair of homonyms for each definition below?

Directors of a corporation who have nothing on their agenda

A wink that
says you agree

This Sir works the
evening shift at the castle.

A postman

A very young antelope

Answers on page 238

Each word below is missing its mate. Can you figure them out?

milk and _____

macaroni and _____

black and _____

right and _____

thunder and _____

SHIRTSHIRTSHIRTSHIRT
SHIRTSHIRTSHIRTSHIRT
SHIRT
SHIRT
SHIRT
SHIRT
SHIRT
SHIRT

Answers on page 238

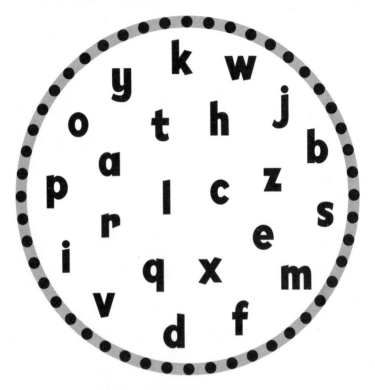

Use the letters of the alphabet that are missing from the circle to find an African antelope.

How to Get Smart by Reed A. Lot

Use Charcoal to Grill by Barb B. Cue

How to Build Sandcastles by Sandy Beech

How to Make Leaves Disappear by Ray Cupp

Answers on page 238

unbiased opinion

liquid gas

act naturally

minor crisis

virtual reality

Picture Puzzler

Palindromes, Please

Was it a bat I saw?

Now I won.

tangy gnat

I prefer pi.

Answers on page 238

Give Mr. Snipe's wife's knife a swipe.

I can think of six thin things and of six thick things too.

an Irish wristwatch

Happy Homonyms

Can you think of a sound-alike for each of these words?

steel

right

seam

prey

Answers on pages 238–239

How to Make a Hole
by Doug Pit

Taking a Test
by B. A. Wiseman

Fun in the Country
by Sid E. Folk

The Perfect S'more by Graham Cracker

Swimming in the Ocean by C. Lyons

Girls Galore is having a sale on everything pink. Can you change PINK into SALE by changing one letter at a time?

PINK

PIN _

PI _ _

P _ _ _

_ _ _ _

Answers on page 239

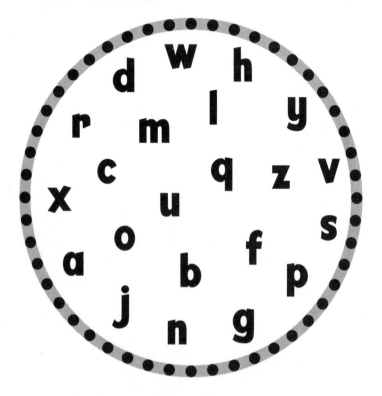

Use the letters of the alphabet that are missing from the circle to find something that flies.

Food that Makes a Party by Cole S. Law

Bargain Shopping by Lois Price

Why Walk? by Iona Carr

The Colors of the Rainbow by Roy G. Biv

Answers on page 239

Unscramble the letters to reveal some things you might pack for vacation.

okbo

storsh

acream

isitswum

snaussgles

What's the Word?

Stgsrs is *Stegosaurus* without its vowels. Can you figure out the names of these other dinosaurs?

Tyrnnsrs rx

Vlcrptr

Trcrtps

72

Oh, Onomatopoeias

crash

jangle

kerplunk

clatter

tsk

ugh

Answers on page 239

sit**ME**

a ppod

this ←
this this
this this this
this this this this
this this this this this

74

Can you remove one letter from
the word *Z E B R A* and rearrange
the remaining letters to spell
another animal?

Answers on page 239

Trent tries to tow his toy truck.

imaginary menagerie manager

Miss Smith's fish-sauce shop

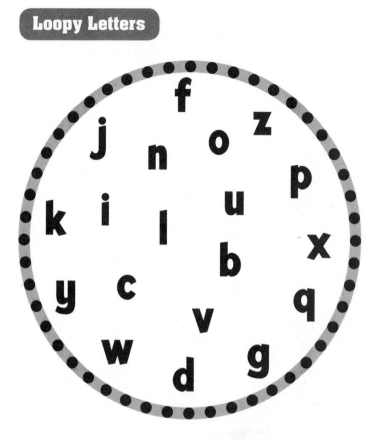

Use the letters of the alphabet that are missing from the circle to find a pet.

Answers on page 239

Can you figure out the names of these ice-cream flavors?

bttr pcn

rcky rd

chclt-chp ck dgh

crml crnch

cks nd crm

If you were to spell out numbers, how far would you have to go until you would find the letter A?

What time is the same spelled backward or forward?

What ten-letter word starts with g-a-s?

Smart People by Gene E. Us

What Usually Happens by General Lee

Under the Sea by Coral Reef

Answers on page 239

flash message

inchworms itching

selfish shellfish

three free throws

preshrunk silk shirts

Twelve twins twirled twelve twigs.

unique New York

river level

Ten tiny turtles sitting on a tiny tin tub turned tan.

Cedar shingles should be shared and saved.

Tim, the thin twin tinsmith

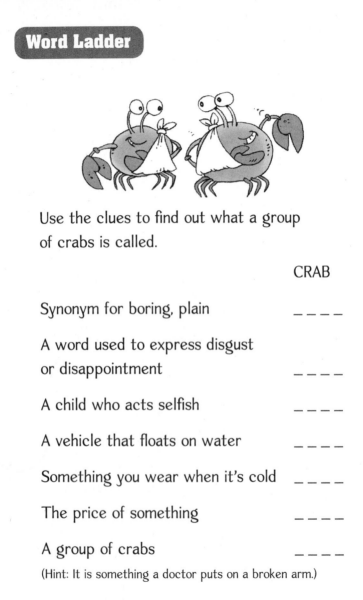

Use the clues to find out what a group
of crabs is called.

	CRAB
Synonym for boring, plain	_ _ _ _
A word used to express disgust or disappointment	_ _ _ _
A child who acts selfish	_ _ _ _
A vehicle that floats on water	_ _ _ _
Something you wear when it's cold	_ _ _ _
The price of something	_ _ _ _
A group of crabs	_ _ _ _

(Hint: It is something a doctor puts on a broken arm.)

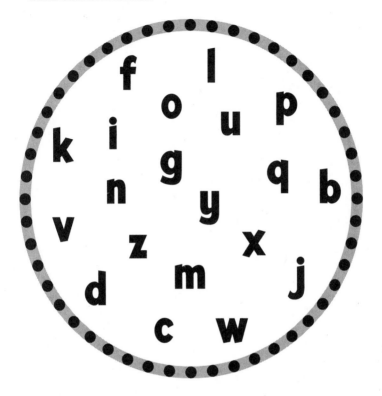

Use the letters of the alphabet that are
missing from the circle to find a card game.

Answers on page 240

Climb the Stairs to Success by Rich N. Famous

Hug Me by Hans Zoff

All-Time Best Novels by Paige Turner

Winning by Lou Singh

Picture Puzzlers

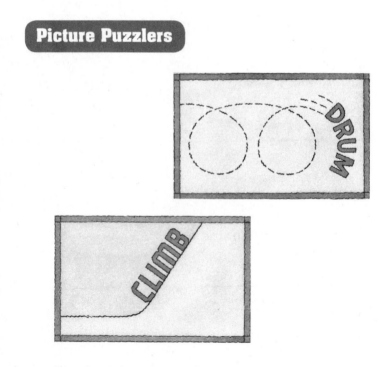

What word can mean:

The front of a boat or to bend forward at the waist

What planes do or a kind of insect

An untruth or something you might do when you're tired

Pretty or reasonable

Answers on page 240

small fortune

forgotten memories

serious fun

long-sleeved T-shirt

never again

Unscramble the letters to reveal the birds.

devo

corw

wkah

nasw

binor

rkost

soeog

eiopgn

tropra

powsrar

uepnign

racildna

Answers on page 240

Each word is the name of a capital city hidden within its home country. Can you find them all?

Canottawaada

Enlondongland

Plimaeru

Franparisce

Jatokyopan

Irometaly

Chavanauba

Spamadridin

What do you see when you look at this cartoon upside down?

Can you think of other words that read the same upside down and right side up?

Answers on page 240

What word can mean:

where pigs are kept
or an ink-filled
writing instrument?

a small, round
serving of bread
or a somersault?

a record of a journey
or a chunk of
a cut-up tree?

to knock lightly or
a faucet spout?

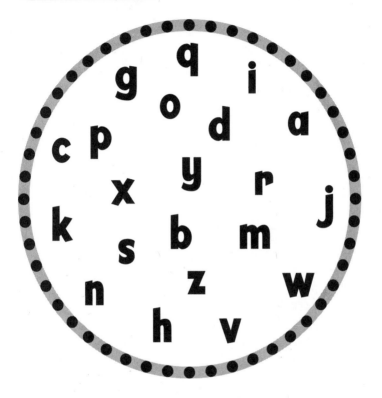

Use the letters of the alphabet that are missing from the circle to find a musical instrument.

Answers on page 241

What's the Word?

Lenny likes sweets, but not chocolate.

Lenny likes rabbits, but not animals.

Lenny likes bass, but not fish.

Can you tell which items on this list Lenny will like and why?

books

bananas

pencils

games

whistles

roses

cards

cameras

money

bills

daffodils

beets

tubas

balloons

tissues

Answers on page 241

well-boiled icicle

damp stealer

talking wall

chewing the doors

Can you think of a homonym for each
of these words?

hall

tale

pole

sent

cruise

flee

Answers on page 241

fingertips = finest grip

clothespins = so let's pinch

rats and mice = in cat's dream

video game = give a demo

astronomers = moon starers

Use the letters of the alphabet that are missing from the circle to find something that keeps you warm outside.

Answers on page 241

Can you find the name of a country hidden in each sentence?

Mom said to give Barb a dose of cough medicine.

We offered Bob a ham as a going-away present.

Sarita is worth her weight in diamonds.

They went to the new spa in the hotel.

Jake has only one pal in this room.

I ran all the way home.

If the gate is stuck, give it a tug and a pull.

Answers on page 241

Oops, Oxymorons

Each sentence contains an oxymoron. Can you spot them? Watch out—some may have two.

"This place seems strangely familiar," the captain declared when the ship pulled into the harbor.

The woman was dismayed to see that the plastic glasses had cracked in the dishwasher.

"I've searched whole hemisphere looking for this dratted treasure!" the pirate exclaimed.

"This is my least favorite cereal!" the boy cried to his mother at the store. "You're a little big to be crying in public," his mother replied.

If you look into the sun at a straight angle, you will hurt your eyes.

After Mandy broke the cookie in half, she gave her little sister the smaller half and gobbled down the bigger half.

Answers on page 241

Tongue Twisters

Sam's shop stocks short spotted socks.

a proper copper coffee pot

rubber baby buggy bumpers

Sheep should sleep in a shed.

no need to light a night light on a light night like tonight

Friendly Frank flips fine flapjacks.

A big black bug bit a big black bear.

girl gargoyle, guy gargoyle

We shall see the sunshine soon.

Whistle for the thistle sifter.

If Stu chews shoes, should Stu choose which shoes he chews?

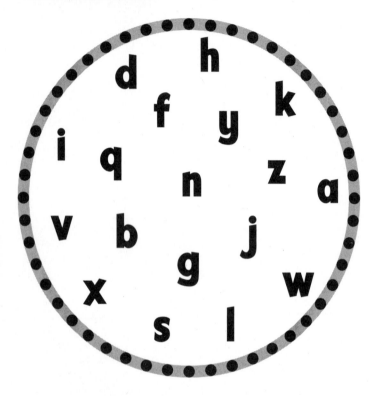

Use the letters of the alphabet that are missing from the circle to find something that helps you learn.

See if you can match the animals to their correct group names.

congregation   butterflies

congress   rattlesnakes

flutter   flamingoes

bed   salamanders

coalition   clams

rhumba   porcupines

flamboyance   cheetahs

prickle   rhinoceroses

crash   alligators

Answers on pages 241–242

all alone

blind eye

burning cold

climb down

cold sweat

extraordinary

fried ice cream

incredibly dull

CA just SE

Oh, Onomatopoeias

snap

rumble

boing

cock-a-doodle-do

ping

trickle

107

Answers on page 242

Which letter of the alphabet is as big as an ocean?

Which letter of the alphabet has a beverage and a shirt named after it?

Which letter of the alphabet is a line of people in England and a stick in billiards?

Which two letters make a clinging vine?

Which two letters make something not difficult?

Which two letters make a prison?

Which three letters make a lot of pep?

Answers on page 242

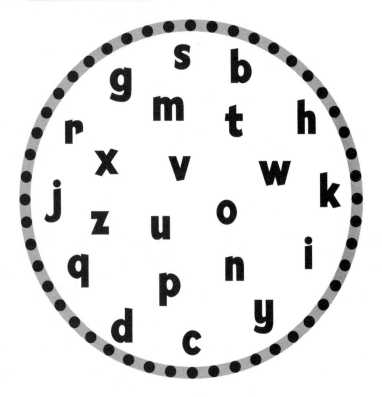

Use the letters of the alphabet that are
missing from the circle to find an annoying
insect.

Palindromes, Please

rotator

pop

solos

eye

racecar

never odd or even

no lemon no melon

Answers on page 242

What's the Word?

Each word described below starts with the letter *b* and ends with *t*. Can you name them?

three-letter words

small piece of something

a flying mammal

a wager

four-letter words

a dark red vegetable

worn on the foot

used for traveling on water

five-letter words

brag

a flat, round hat

a sudden loud sound

Answers on page 242

"Sissy as a nana," says sis.

pot top

wet stew

Yo, banana boy!

Step on no pets.

Answers on page 242

Golf

every RIGHT thing

CLOWN

Unscramble the words to reveal the animals.

fullborg

somsupo

kendoy

ricecoldo

aknargoo

Answers on page 242

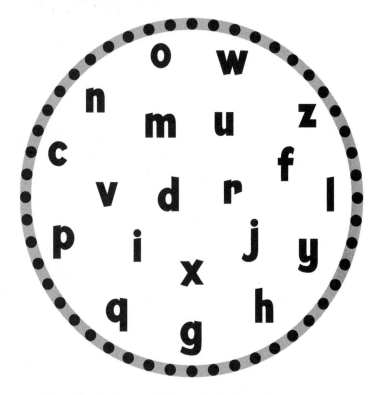

Use the letters of the alphabet that are missing from the circle to find something you take on a picnic.

Mr. See owned a saw.

And Mr. Soar owned a seesaw.

Now See's saw sawed Soar's seesaw

Before Soar saw See,

Which made Soar sore.

Had Soar seen See's saw

Before See sawed Soar's seesaw,

See's saw would not have sawed

Soar's seesaw.

Answers on page 242

119

These state capitals have been turned into spoonerisms. Can you figure out each capital—and its state?

Miss Bark

Lono Hulu

Hallatassee

Tosbon

Vender

WELCOME TO LONO HULU!

Fanta Se

Riddle Lock

Paint Saul

Sack John

Answers on page 242

See if you can make one or more new words from the letters of each word below.

stew

thorn

deal

owl

kids

123

Answers on page 243

Where's the Word?

Can you find the name of a country hidden in each sentence?

This pain in my elbow is annoying.

I bought a rug and a lamp at the yard sale.

Is jazz music way in or way out?

YaRD SaLe

Answers on page 243

Here's how to write your own tongue twister:

Think of words that begin with the first letter of your name—then string them together.

Example: Sally saw six steep slopes.

Challenge: Can you come up with rhyming words for your tongue twister?

Example: Silly Sally saw a hilly valley.

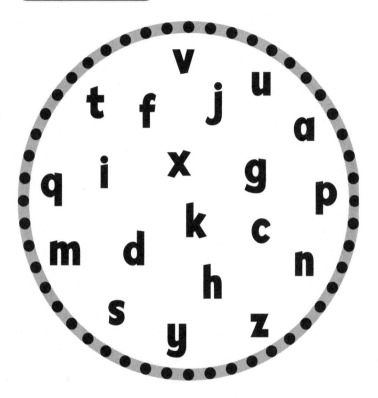

Use the letters of the alphabet that are missing from the circle to find a type of hat.

Answers on page 243

The World According to Pigs by Ima Hog

Great Breakfast Recipes by Pam Cake

How to Get Rid of a Cold by Anita Tizzue

Eat Your Veggies by Brock A. Lee

Answers on page 243

Try reading this aloud.

A tree toad loved a she-toad

Who lived up in a tree.

He was a two-toed tree toad

But a three-toed toad was she.

The two-toed tree toad tried to win

The three-toed she-toad's heart,

For the two-toed tree toad loved the ground

That the three-toed tree toad trod.

But the two-toed tree toad tried in vain.

He couldn't please her whim.

From her tree-toad bower

With her three-toed power

The she-toad vetoed him.

Oops, Oxymorons

Pair the answer to the clue on the left with the answer to the clue on the right to make an oxymoron. See if you can get them all.

The temperature in the summertime	Something you might put on a hot dog

Where you keep ice cream	What you get when you touch something hot

Opposite of young	Tells you what is happening in the world

Answers on page 243

Good Housekeeping by Dustin D. Houss

Favorite Fall Flowers by Chris-Ann T. Mums

Bouncing Off Walls by Rick O. Shea

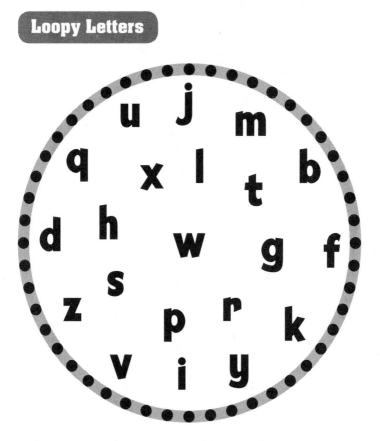

Use the letters of the alphabet that are missing from the circle to find something that travels on water.

Answers on page 243

nosy little cook

a blushing crow

tons of soil

know your blows

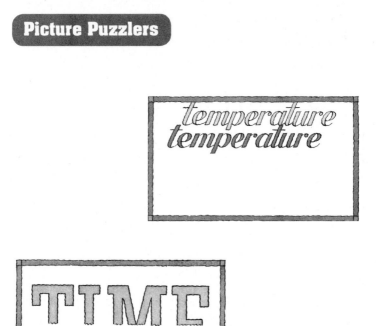

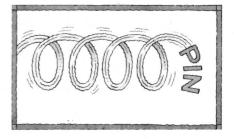

Answers on page 243

Can you figure out the names of these birds?

cnry

gldfnch

prrt

hwk

gl

Where's the Word?

Find the fruit hidden in each sentence.

Is it chocolate or angel food cake?

No one can ban a nation.

Pile money up high.

Wear a cap, please.

I tied rope around the fence.

Improve Your Vision with Glasses
by Dr. I. C. Better

Fibs I've Told by Liza Little

Liking Yourself by Ima Goodgirl

Grub Recipes of the Frontier by Chuck Wagon

Answers on page 244

WONaDIEiRcLeAND

JACK

BAN ANA

Word Ladder

Can you change FOOD into BOWL?

FOOD

_ _ _ _

_ _ _ _

BOWL

Anagram Antics

the detectives = detect thieves

listen = silent

conversation = voices rant on

butterfly = flutter by

Answers on page 244

Take a look at these doctors' names. Which of them are palindromes?

Absurd Dr. Usba

Bearded Dr. Dedreab

Dr. Awkward

Drab Dr. D. Bard

Bored Dr. Gourd

Doctor E. Rotcod

Doctor Chopper

Silly Dr. Yills

Tiny Dr. Dynit

Answers on page 244

143

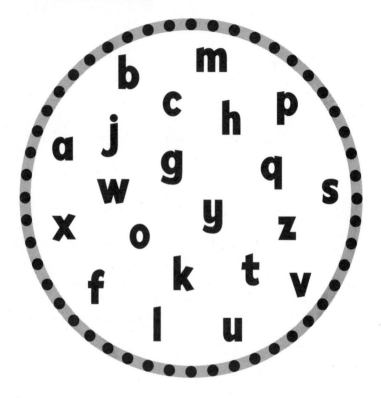

Use the letters of the alphabet that are missing from the circle to find where to get a bite to eat.

Early humans made rocks into tools. Can you do the same?

ROCK

_ _ _ _

_ _ _ _

TOOL

Answers on page 244

You can get milk from cows but can you get cows from milk? Figure it out by using the clues.

MILK

5,280 feet   _ _ _ _

A marsh or a bog   _ _ _ _

To employ someone   _ _ _ _

Opposite of there   _ _ _ _

Belonging to a woman   _ _ _ _

Cuts down with an ax   _ _ _ _

Sounds kittens make   _ _ _ _

Cuts the lawn   _ _ _ _

COWS

Can you think of sound-alikes for these words?

scene

which

browse

err

buoy

cell

feat

grown

Answers on pages 244–245

Swan swam over the sea—swim, swan, swim.
Swan swam back again—well swum, swan.

Funny Freddy Flanders fell face first fixing
faucets for friends.

Ed had edited it.

Crisp crusts crackle crunchily.

Please pay promptly.

Lesser leather never weathered.

Elvis = lives

snooze alarms = alas, no more Z's

naturalist = a trails nut

the countryside = no city dust here

Six shaved sheep shivered silently.

What kind of noise annoys an oyster?

Pigs play pinball at pizza palaces.

Answers on page 245

Pink panthers prance proudly.

Two timid tree toads tied together tried
to trot to town.

Which wristwatch is a Swiss wristwatch?

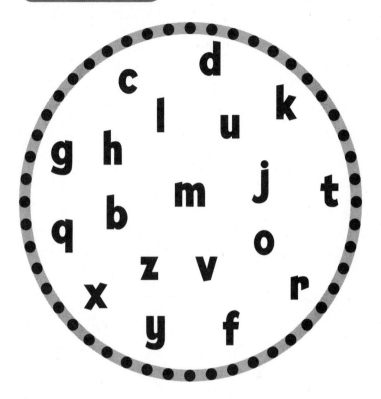

Use the letters of the alphabet that are missing from the circle to find a type of apple.

Answers on page 245

Each of these sentences is missing a color. What are they?

I think I'll go _____ and recycle.

Why, you _____-bellied, lily-livered cowards!

Aha! I caught you _____-handed.

He was tickled _____ to hear the news.

That just happened out of the _____!

The proud soldier was awarded a ___ Heart.

What letter of the alphabet is always difficult to figure out?

Why is the letter T like an island?

How do you spell hard water with three letters?

Answers on page 245

Sound out each puzzle to find a place that ends with the letter *O*.

1. + + (- yo) = ?

2. + (- ck) + = ?

3. (- g) + + O = ?

4.  + O = ?

5. ( - tle) + (- f) + = ?

6. (- op) + X + (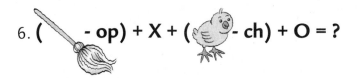 - ch) + O = ?

7. pw + (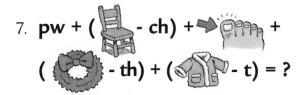 - ch) + +
(- th) + (- t) = ?

Answers on page 245

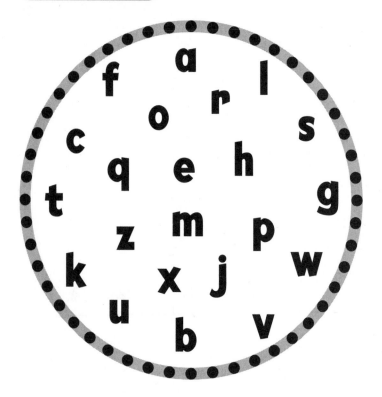

Use the letters of the alphabet that are missing from the circle to find a skateboarding trick.

How Big Are Elephants? by Hugh Mongus

Cowboy Lassos by Larry Ett

How to Get Clean by Anita Bath

Answers on page 245

*See if you can read this aloud
without stumbling.*

I brought a big basket of biscuits back to the

bakery and baked a basket of big biscuits.

Then I took the big basket of biscuits and the

basket of big biscuits and mixed the big

biscuits with the basket of biscuits that was

next to the big basket and put a batch of

biscuits from the basket into a box. Then I took

the big basket of biscuits and the biscuit mixer

and the biscuit basket and brought to the

bakery the basket of biscuits and the box of

mixed biscuits and the biscuit mixer and took

the biscuit mixer home.

nothing much

still moving

rude welcome

now, then

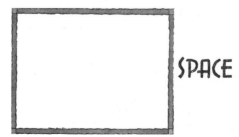

163

Answers on page 245

Can you change FISH into MASK?

FISH

_ _ _ _

_ _ _ _

_ _ _ _

MASK

The two clues in each question each give half of a palindrome phrase. Put the two answers together to get the whole phrase.

Example: Enthusiastic or vigorous/A glamorous female performer

Answer: avid diva

1. Something you might get for a good deed/A place to keep silverware

2. Something you can cook in/The opposite of bottom

3. An animal with feathers/Something you might eat at a barbecue

4. Not smart/Mixture of water and dirt

Answers on pages 245–246

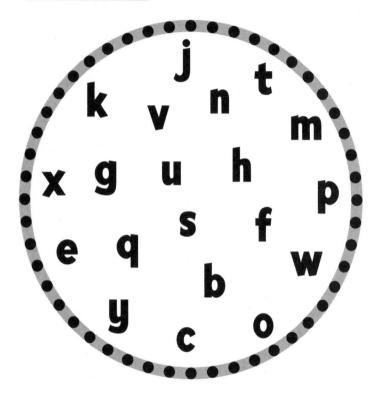

Use the letters of the alphabet that are
missing from the circle to find something
with a long tongue.

Can you figure out the names of these pizza toppings?

mshrms

chs

ppprn

nchvs

nn

pnppl

ssg

bll pppr

grlc

tmt sc

Answers on page 246

Figure out what word is missing from these common phrases.

Great minds think ____.

A taste of your own _____

A dime a _____

_____ speak louder than words.

Curiosity killed the ___.

_____ a leg.

_____ is of the essence.

Cut to the _____.

Beat around the _____.

Answers on page 246

The bottom of the butter bucket is the buttered bucket bottom.

If two witches were watching two watches, which witch would watch which watch?

Pete Brigg's pink pig's big pig's pigpen.

Unscramble the words to reveal the bugs.

kict

thom

debubg

graphposers

leeteb

leaf

kitcrec

sootquim

Picture Puzzler

Answers on page 246

Palindromes, Please

non

tot

oho

gag

level

deed

dad

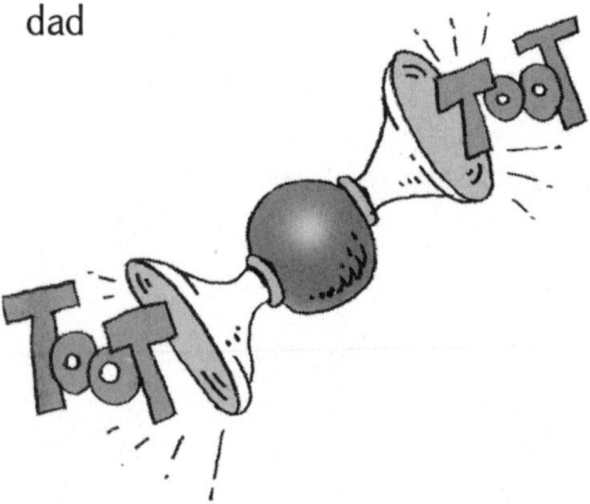

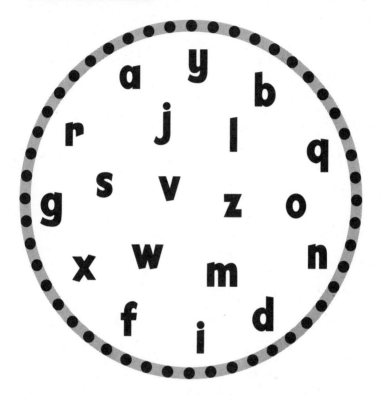

Use the letters of the alphabet that are missing from the circle to find something to put on a hamburger.

Answers on page 247

Unscramble the letters to find the space words.

rams

metco

unrats

ritbo

lymik yaw

clabk loeh

tipjuer

dreatsio

snveu

174

What word when spelled forward is heavy but when spelled backward is not?

What word doesn't belong in this group?
That, hat, what, mat, cat, sat, pat, or *chat?*

What unusual property do the words *flour, tern,* and *thirsty* have in common?

 Answers on page 247

chipping the flannel

shake a tower

bunny phone

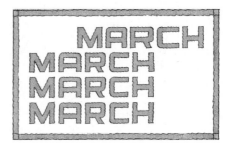

Answers on page 247

Can you think of a sound-alike for each
of these words?

meat

pail

steal

peace

waist

sail

weak

fore

rose

rap

ring

our

fairy

knot

toe

Each puzzle adds up to a country's capital city.
Can you name each country, too?

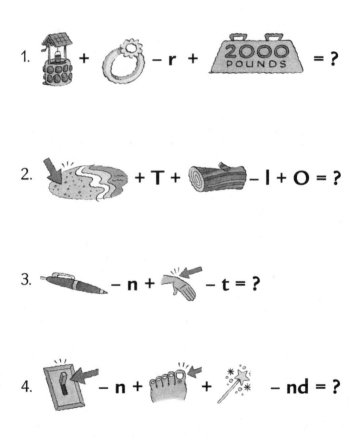

1. [well] + [ring] − r + [2000 POUNDS] = ?

2. [beach] + T + [log] − l + O = ?

3. [pen] − n + [hand] − t = ?

4. [switch] − n + [toe] + [wand] − nd = ?

Palindromes, Please

A car, a man, a maraca!

Dee saw a seed.

No sir! Away! A papaya war is on.

So, cat tacos!

A Santa at NASA.

Answers on page 247

Unscramble the words to reveal the animals.

chowdouck

peesh

paderol

somue

kegco

fabfulo

raplo ebar

Can you change ROCK into LOOP?

ROCK

_ _ _ _

_ _ _ _

LOOP

Answers on page 248

Can you guess the meanings of these words?

spelunking

cockamamie

caddywampus

flibbertigibbet

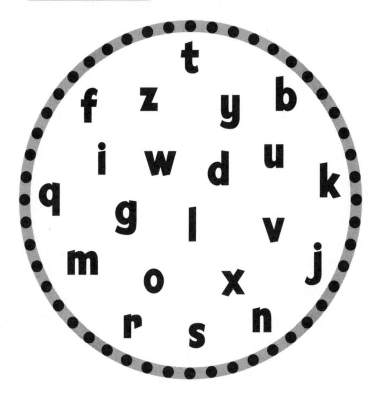

Use the letters of the alphabet that are
missing from the circle to find a juicy fruit.

Answers on page 248

A word is hidden on each line below. You can find it by skipping every other letter. The first one shows you how.

d e a r i p s l y = daisy

1. f l i p f o t r y

2. s a l e i o n e g

3. f u l e a r k l e

4. s e t t i n c u k

5. b l o t o s k i s

Pronounced as one letter,

And written with three,

Two letters there are,

And two only in me.

I'm double, I'm single, I'm brown, blue, and gray,

I'm read from both ends,

And the same either way.

What am I?

What's the Word?

Can you figure out the names of these insects?

> bttrfly
>
> msqt
>
> ldybg
>
> bmblb
>
> nt

Answers on page 248

Where's the Word?

Can you spot the state name in each sentence?

The radio wasn't tuned in very well.

Superstitious Sid slid a horseshoe into his desk.

I've been washing tons of clothes today.

Esther plans to color a dozen eggs for the party.

It's just exasperating to be kept waiting.

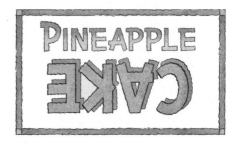

Answers on page 248

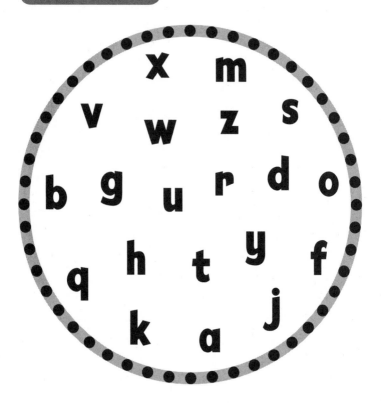

Use the letters of the alphabet that are missing from the circle to find something you use at school.

Frank fried fresh frankfurters
for forty-four men.

frozen fuzzy feet

Granny grabbed a Grammy.

Answers on page 248

Grover the Grocer ran out of melons, so he was going to throw away this sign. Then he realized that he could switch just two of the letters to make a sign for his latest shipment of fruit. What fruit will he advertise?

Answers on pages 248–249

Few free fruit flies fly from flames.

magnificent musicianship

Paula picks pink paper.

Take a look at these squares. Each word can be
read up, down, across, and backwards.
Try your hand at creating a palindrome square.

```
N E T        Y A M        P O T

E Y E        A H A        O H O

T E N        M A Y        T O P
```

Each answer contains the word *big* or *little*.

What is the capital of Arkansas?

What is the main tent in a circus often called?

Who is the title character—a mouse—in a popular book by E. B. White?

What is the children's story about a train engine who believes in herself?

What is a nutritious-sounding nickname for New York City?

Answers on page 249

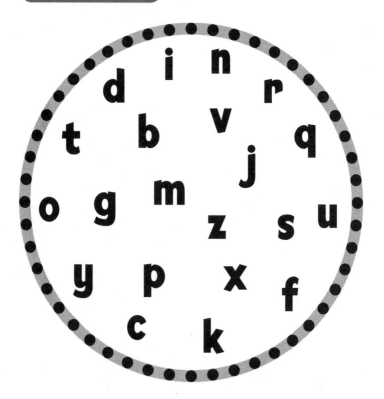

Use the letters of the alphabet that are missing from the circle to find a mammal that lives in the ocean.

Landscaping Tips by Pete Moss

The King Who Could Not Fall Asleep
by Eliza Wake

Into the Dark Forest by Hugo First

Let's Go Home! by Dewey Havta

Answers on page 249

Tongue Twisters

Pick a partner and practice passing. If you pass proficiently pehaps you'll play professionally.

The blue bluebird blinks.

Draw drowsy ducks and drakes.

What's the Word?

Can you figure out the names of these bicycle parts?

hndlbr

spks

whls

brks

grs

Safe Road Crossing by Luke Left
and Den Wright

City Slickers by Letz B. Farmers

Sing Out Loud by Mike Rophone

How to Cook Pasta by Lynne Guini

Answers on page 249

How to be Neat by Mae K. Mess

Bad Communications by Lowden Clear

Soil: Dig In! by Hans R. Durtie

How to Put in Seedlings by Neil N. Plant

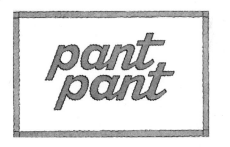

Answers on page 249

Something is not quite right with each of these sayings. Can you fix them?

It'll cost an arm and a tooth!

Oh, they come a quarter a dozen.

I don't understand that report.
It's all English to me.

Let's go back to the cutting board.

Wow, he's squeaky rich!

That's easy as carrots!

Hold your pigs! I'm coming!

Answers on page 249

buzz

sob

drip

swish

thump

tick tock

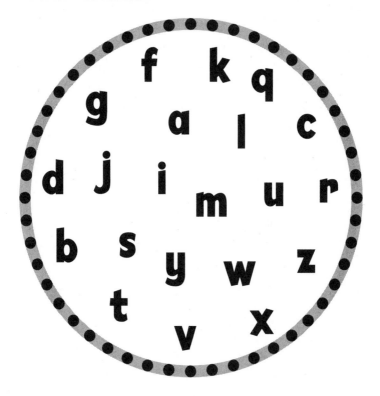

Use the letters of the alphabet that are missing from the circle to find a way to keep in touch.

207

Answers on page 249

Can you figure out the names of these clothes?

sspndrs

tnk tp

vrlls

jns

jckt

Picture Puzzler

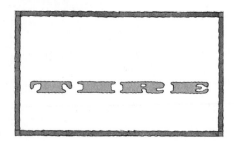

Can you guess the meanings of these words?

lackadaisical

discombobulated

hobnob

I THINK I'LL HAVE ANOTHER SNICKERDOODLE.

flabbergasted

snickerdoodle

gobbledygook

harbinger

Answers on pages 249–250

Unscramble the letters to reveal the trees.

lawtun

ryrech

nipe

chrib

pleam

raced

owlwil

koa

Each word is missing its mate. Can you figure them out?

salt and _____

fire and _____

rock and _____

socks and _____

chips and _____

Answers on page 250

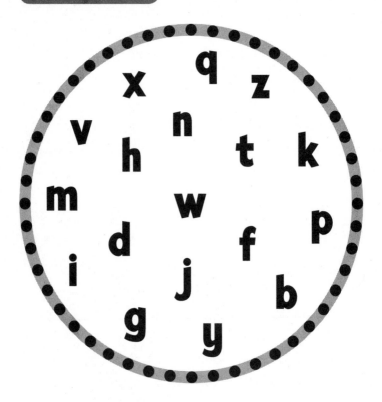

Use the letters of the alphabet that are
missing from the circle to find something
fun to ride.

Can you guess the meanings of these words?

boondoggle

bamboozle

hootenanny

bumbershoot

Answers on page 250

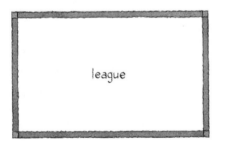

meat team

I'm a fool; aloof am I.

dumb mud

reward drawer

215

Answers on page 250

Can you untangle these sentences?

I took my walk for a dog so he could catch a park in the stick.

I here am but where you are?

This street has so many cities! My tired are feet.

It's Going to Rain by Zeke Shelter

The Haunted House by N. E. Bodie Home

Healthy Eating by Kara Mell

How to Wash a Dog by Al Wet

Answers on page 251

rental deceptionist

mad banners

plaster man

birthington's washday

Find the valuable word that is missing from each phrase.

heart of _____

_____ medal

All that glitters is not _____.

219

Answers on page 251

toy boat

many an anemone enemy

six sharp smart sharks

lovely lemony lozenges

red leather, yellow leather

rubber baby-buggy bumpers

What letter makes each design?

1.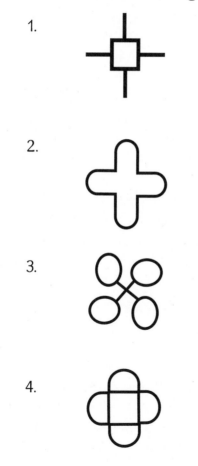

2.

3.

4.

After School by Dee Tension

Downpour by Wayne Dwops

How to Catch Worms by Earl E. Bird

Places to Exercise by Jim Nasium

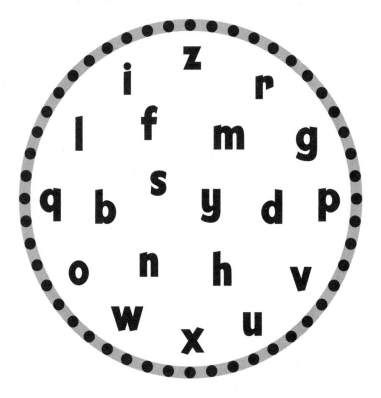

Use the letters of the alphabet that are missing from the circle to find something to wear.

Answers on page 251

the railroad train = Hi! I rattle and roar.

waitress = A stew, sir?

postmaster = stamp store

the hurricanes = These churn air.

a decimal point = I'm a dot in place.

fir cones = conifers

hot water = worth tea

vacation time = I am not active.

Picture Puzzler

READING

Answers on page 251

stand

Can you change FEW into something more?
Start from the bottom and follow the clues.

_ _ _ _ add one letter

_ _ _ a human male; change one letter

_ _ _ a light brown color; change one letter

_ _ _ the number of toes on your feet; change
one letter

_ _ _ a female chicken; change one letter

_ _ _ the opposite of women; drop one letter
and change one letter

_ _ _ _ the sound a cat makes; add one letter

_ _ _ to cut grass; change one letter

_ _ _ right this minute; change one letter

_ _ _ the opposite of old; change one letter

FEW

Answers on page 251

The Best Doctor by Ophelia Pain

Check Your Reflexes by Ben Journee

The Coldest Continent by Aunt Arctica

An Encyclopedia of Monsters by Frank N. Stein

How to Be an Actor by Holly Wood

Meeting Deadlines by Justin Time

Answers on page 252

Can you figure out these homonym groups from the clues?

A female deer and unbaked bread

A coat for a pet and a type of tree

A group of musical notes played together and something you plug in

A female sheep, a type of tree, and the opposite of me

A synonym for oceans, when you take something, and what your eye does

Answers on page 252

Don't Get Lost in the Forest! by Mark deTrayle

Preparing Vegetables by Shel d'Peeze

Easy Composting by Lettie Trott

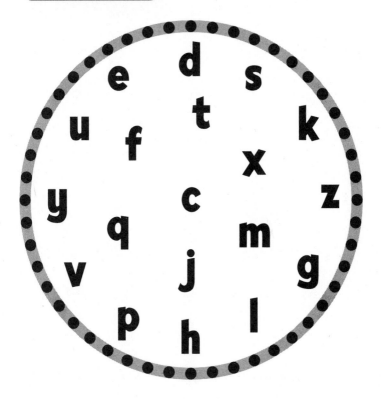

Use the letters of the alphabet that are missing from the circle to find something beautiful in the sky.

Answers on page 252

Answers

2 What's the Word?
Letters can be strange.

Picture Puzzler
trail mix

5 Loopy Letters
quack

6 Picture Puzzlers
first down
shots on goal
hole in one

7 Scrambled Words
soup
taco
stew
steak
chili
salad
burger
stir-fry

8 Loony Spoonerisms
dear friends
My lips are zipped.
lighting a fire

9 Loopy Letters
hockey

11 Word Ladder
DOGS
DOTS
COTS
CATS

13 Loopy Letters
wrench

15 Riddle-Dee-Dee
seeing a goldfish bowl
the letter *T*
alphabet

16 Picture Puzzlers
center of attention
splitting hairs
strong undertow

17 Loony Spoonerisms
bunny rabbit
save the whales
mad as a hatter
loving shepherd

19 Loopy Letters
leopard

Answers

20 Rebus Riot
1. Stockholm, Sweden
2. Nairobi, Kenya
3. Rome, Italy
4. Budapest, Hungary

21 Riddle-Dee-Dee
H, I, and M can be drawn
using only straight lines.
H, I, S, and O look the same
right side up or upside down.

22 Riddle-Dee-Dee
the letter *I*

23 Picture Puzzler
Think outside the box.

24 What's the Word?
fever of stingrays
army of frogs
pod of whales
streak of tigers
tower of giraffes
kine of cows
leap of leopards
plague of locusts

25 Loopy Letters
candy

26 Picture Puzzlers
1. M
2. Z
3. E
4. G

28–29 What's the Word?
Vermont
Alaska
Connecticut
Alabama
North Carolina
Ohio

30 Loopy Letters
weak

33 Scrambled Words
tennis
football
lacrosse
baseball
hockey
soccer
gymnastics
volleyball
swimming
basketball
karate

Answers

34 Riddle-Dee-Dee

Most English language
sources say that there
are no words that rhyme
exactly with any of these
words.
empty (MT)

37 Picture Puzzler

three strikes and you're out

39 Loopy Letters

Saturn

42 Picture Puzzlers

ten seconds
sleep tight
rock 'n' roll

43 What's the Word?

bill
orange
nail
lace
coat

45 Loopy Letters

island

46–47 Happy Homonyms

peak/peek
aloud/allowed
poor/pour
bite/byte
flu/flew
close/clothes
one/won
horse/hoarse
some/sum
plain/plane

Picture Puzzler

top left

48 Riddle-Dee-Dee

forty
Y—It is one-fourth of YARD.
an envelope containing
   a letter
few
C and Y

50 Loony Spoonerisms

pouring rain
handle with care
bye, all
speed of light

51 Picture Puzzlers
right behind you
last chance
swing set

53 What's the Word?
canary
volcano
candle
pecan
canoe

Picture Puzzler
dinner for two

55 Picture Puzzlers
first place
right around the corner
leftovers

56–57 Palindromes, Please
redder
kayak
rotator

Picture Puzzlers
fast food
poetry in motion

58–59 Happy Homonyms
bored/board
eye/aye
night/knight
mail/male
new/gnu

60 What's the Word?
milk and cookies
macaroni and cheese
black and white
right and left
thunder and lightning

61 Picture Puzzlers
Sign on the dotted line.
once in a while
T-shirt

62 Loopy Letters
gnu

64 Picture Puzzler
raisin bread (rays in bread)

66 Happy Homonyms
steel/steal
right/write
seam/seem
prey/pray

67 Picture Puzzlers
handshake
comedy
She's on cloud nine.

69 Word Ladder
PINK
PINE
PILE
PALE
SALE

Picture Puzzler
Repeat after me.

70 Loopy Letters
kite

72 Scrambled Words
book
shorts
camera
swimsuit
sunglasses

What's the Word?
Tyrannosaurus rex
Velociraptor
Triceratops

74 Picture Puzzlers
Sit in front of me.
two peas in a pod
Top this.

75 Scrambled Words
Remove the *Z* to form *bear*.

77 Loopy Letters
hamster

78 What's the Word?
butter pecan
rocky road
chocolate-chip cookie
dough
caramel crunch
cookies and cream

Riddle-Dee-Dee
one thousand
noon
automobile

Answers

82 Word Ladder

CRAB
DRAB
DRAT
BRAT
BOAT
COAT
COST
CAST

83 Loopy Letters

Hearts

84 Picture Puzzlers

drum roll
uphill climb

85 What's the Word?

bow
fly
lie
fair

87 Scrambled Words

dove
crow
hawk
swan
robin
stork
goose
pigeon
parrot
sparrow
penguin
cardinal

88 Where's the Word?

Ottawa, Canada
London, England
Lima, Peru
Paris, France
Tokyo, Japan
Rome, Italy
Havana, Cuba
Madrid, Spain

89 Palindromes, Please

We thought of NOON, SIS,
and SWIMS. You may have
thought of others.

Answers

90 What's the Word?
pen
roll
log
tap

91 Loopy Letters
flute

92-93 What's the Word?
Lenny likes words that have
two of the same letter in a
row: books, bills, daffodils,
beets, balloons, and tissues.

94 Loony Spoonerisms
well-oiled bicycle
stamp dealer
walking tall
doing the chores

95 Happy Homonyms
hall/haul
tale/tail
pole/poll
sent/cent
cruise/crews
flee/flea

Picture Puzzler
Little House on the Prairie

97 Loopy Letters
campfire

98-99 Where's the Word?
Barbados
Bahamas
India
Spain
Nepal
Iran
Uganda

100-101 Oops, Oxymorons
strangely familiar
plastic glasses
whole hemisphere
least favorite
little big
straight angle
smaller half
bigger half

104 Loopy Letters
computer

Answers

105 What's the Word?

congregation of alligators
congress of salamanders
flutter of butterflies
bed of clams
coalition of cheetahs
rhumba of rattlesnakes
flamboyance of flamingoes
prickle of porcupines
crash of rhinoceroses

107 Picture Puzzler

just in case

108–109 Riddle-Dee-Dee

C (sea)
T (tea and T-shirt)
Q (queue and cue)
IV (ivy)
EZ (easy)
JL (jail)
NRG (energy)

110 Loopy Letters

Flea

112–113 What's the Word?

bit, bat, bet
beet, boot, boat
boast, beret, blast

114 Picture Puzzlers

shortstop
flag on the play
taking the field

116 Picture Puzzlers

miniature golf
right in the middle
   of everything
clown around

117 Scrambled Words

bullfrog
opossum
donkey
crocodile
kangaroo

118 Loopy Letters

basket

120–121 Loony Spoonerisms

Bismarck, North Dakota
Honolulu, Hawaii
Tallahassee, Florida
Boston, Massachusetts
Denver, Colorado
Santa Fe, New Mexico
Little Rock, Arkansas
Saint Paul, Minnesota
Jackson, Mississippi

122 Anagram Antics

Here are the words we found. You may have found others.
stew: west
thorn: north
deal: lead, dale
owl: low
kids: skid

123 Picture Puzzlers

big cheese
comic strips
second grade

124 Where's the Word?

Spain
Uganda
Norway

127 Loopy Letters

bowler

128 Picture Puzzlers

wake up
skating on thin ice
three o'clock

132 Oops, Oxymorons

hot chili
freezer burn
old news

135 Loopy Letters

canoe

136 Loony Spoonerisms

cozy little nook
a crushing blow
sons of toil
blow your nose

137 Picture Puzzlers

rising temperatures
half time
rolling pin

Answers

244

147 Happy Homonyms
scene/seen
which/witch
browse/brows
err/air
buoy/boy
cell/sell
feat/feet
grown/groan

Picture Puzzler
Bigfoot

151 Picture Puzzlers
the White House
the day before yesterday
roundup

153 Loopy Letters
Winesap

154 What's the Word?
green
yellow
red
pink
blue
purple

155 Riddle-Dee-Dee
Y
It's in the middle of water.
I-C-E

156–157 Rebus Riot
Tokyo
Idaho
Morocco
Colorado
Toronto
Mexico
Puerto Rico

158 Loopy Letters
indy

163 Picture Puzzlers
sea level
minute by minute
outer space

164 Word Ladder
FISH
DISH
DASH
MASH
MASK

Answers

165 Palindromes, Please
reward drawer
pot top
bird rib
dumb mud

166 Loopy Letters
lizard

167 What's the Word?
mushrooms
cheese
pepperoni
anchovies
onion
pineapple
sausage
bell pepper
garlic
tomato sauce

168-169 What's the Word?
Great minds think alike.
A taste of your own
    medicine
A dime a dozen
Actions speak louder
    than words.
Curiosity killed the cat.
Break a leg.
Time is of the essence.
Cut to the chase.
Beat around the bush.

171 Scrambled Words
tick
moth
bedbug
grasshopper
beetle
flea
cricket
mosquito

Picture Puzzler
fading away

173 Loopy Letters

ketchup

174 Scrambled Words

Mars
comet
Saturn
orbit
Milky Way
black hole
Jupiter
asteroid
Venus

Picture Puzzler

big fuss over nothing

175 Riddle-Dee-Dee

ton

What doesn't belong. All
the other words rhyme.
When you remove one
letter from each word,
each spells a numeral—
four, ten, and thirty.

176 Loony Spoonerisms

flipping the channel
take a shower
funny bone

177 Picture Puzzlers

high time
mashed potatoes
march out of step

178–179 Happy Homonyms

meat/meet
pail/pale
steal/steel
peace/piece
waist/waste
sail/sale
weak/week
fore/four
rose/rows
rap/wrap
ring/wring
our/hour
fairy/ferry
knot/not
toe/tow

180 Rebus Riot

Wellington, New Zealand
Santiago, Chile
Paris, France
Ottawa, Canada

Answers

182 Scrambled Words

woodchuck
sheep
leopard
mouse
gecko
buffalo
polar bear

183 Word Ladder

ROCK
LOCK
LOOK
LOOP

184 Wacky Words

spelunking: cave exploring
cockamamie: absurd
caddywampus: crooked
flibbertigibbet: a silly
  person

185 Loopy Letters

Peach

186 Where's the Word?

fifty
sling
flake
stick
books

187 Riddle-Dee-Dee

an eye

What's the Word?

butterfly
mosquito
ladybug
bumblebee
ant

188 Where's the Word?

Iowa
Idaho
Washington
Colorado
Texas

189 Picture Puzzlers

pineapple upside-down
  cake
just between you and me
too many cooks

190 Loopy Letters

pencil

192 What's the Word?

By switching the *M* and
  the *L* on the sign,
  Grover can advertise
  LEMONS.

Answers

193 Picture Puzzlers
crossroads
one in a million

196–197 What's the Word?
Little Rock
big top
Stuart Little
*The Little Engine
    That Could*
Big Apple

198 Loopy Letters
whale

200 What's the Word?
handlebar
spokes
wheels
brakes
gears

203 Picture Puzzlers
once (ones) upon a time
pair of pants
batter up

204–205 What's the Word?
It'll cost an arm and a leg!
Oh, they come a dime a
    dozen.
It's all Greek to me.
Let's go back to the
    drawing board.
Wow, he's filthy rich!
That's easy as pie!
Hold your horses!

207 Loopy Letters
phone

208 What's the Word?
suspenders
tank top
overalls
jeans
jacket

Picture Puzzler
flat tire

Answers

209 **Wacky Words**

lackadaisical: carelessly lazy

discombobulated: confused

hobnob: to socialize

flabbergasted: astonished

snickerdoodle: a type of cookie

gobbledygook: nonsense

harbinger: one that announces or shows what is coming

210 **Scrambled Words**

walnut

cherry

pine

birch

maple

cedar

willow

oak

Picture Puzzler

head over heels

211 **What's the Word?**

salt and pepper

fire and ice

rock and roll

socks and shoes

chips and dip

212 **Loopy Letters**

carousel

213 **Wacky Words**

boondoggle: a wasteful project

bamboozle: to deceive

hootenanny: a folk music event

bumbershoot: umbrella

214 **Picture Puzzlers**

half past four

Little League

slightly overcast

Answers

216 Scrambled Words

I took my dog for a walk so he could catch a stick in the park.

Here I am, but where are you?

This city has so many streets! My feet are tired.

217 Picture Puzzler

all mixed up

218 Loony Spoonerisms

dental receptionist

bad manners

master plan

Washington's birthday

219 What's the Word?

heart of gold

gold medal

All that glitters is not gold.

Picture Puzzler

long underwear

221 Picture Puzzlers

T

U

Q

D

223 Loopy Letters

jacket

225 Picture Puzzler

reading between the lines

226 Picture Puzzlers

coast to coast

the inside story

stand in line

227 Word Ladder

MANY

MAN

TAN

TEN

HEN

MEN

MEOW

MOW

NOW

NEW

FEW

Answers

229 Picture Puzzlers
all-star game
full count
third quarter

230-231 Happy Homonyms
doe/dough
fur/fir
chord/cord
ewe/yew/you
seas/seize/sees

Picture Puzzler
square dance

233 Loopy Letters
rainbow